Dante or Die

Skin Hunger

A socially distant performance installation

With writing by Ann Akinjirin, Tim Crouch and Sonia Hughes

@danteordie
www.danteordie.com

Salamander Street

PLAYS

First published in 2021 by Salamander Street Ltd, 272 Bath Street, Glasgow, G2 4JR

info@salamanderstreet.com / www.salamanderstreet.com

Copyright: Dante or Die, Ann Akinjirin, Tim Crouch & Sonia Hughes, 2021

Dante or Die, Ann Akinjirin, Tim Crouch & Sonia Hughes are hereby identified as co-authors of this piece in accordance with section 77 of the Copyright, Designs and Patents Act 1988. The authors have asserted their moral rights.

All rights whatsoever in this play are strictly reserved and application for professional performance should be made to Dante or Die Ltd, Stone Nest, 136 Shaftesbury Avenue, London W1D 5EZ, UK (attn Terry O'Donovan terry@danteordie.com / Daphna Attias daphna@danteordie.com) and for amateur performance etc to Salamander Street Ltd. No performance may be given unless a license has been obtained.

You may not copy, store, distribute, transmit, reproduce or otherwise make available this publication (or any part of it) in any form, or binding or by any means (print, electronic, digital, optical, mechanical, photocopying, recording or otherwise), without the prior written permission of the publisher. Any person who does any unauthorised act in relation to this publication may be liable to criminal prosecution and civil claims for damages.

PB ISBN 9781914228292

E ISBN 9781914228285

Cover image: Justin Jones

Contents

Foreword by Professor Francis McGlone, Research Centre in Brain & Behaviour, Liverpool John Moores University	p.5
About Dante or Die	p.7
Original Production Credits	p.8
Introduction by Daphna Attias – Co-Artistic Director & Director	p.10
The Production	p.14
Reflection by Ann Akinjirin – Writer	p.29
Our Hands by Ann Akinjirin	p.32
Reflection by Ayse Tashkiran – Movement Director	p.41
Reflection by Tim Crouch – Writer	p.44
The Sessions by Tim Crouch	p.49
Reflection by Terry O'Donovan – Co-Artistic Director & Performer	p.54
Reflection by Sonia Hughes – Writer	p.57
Touch the Flesh by Sonia Hughes	p.60
Reflection from The Audience	p.68

Foreword by Professor Francis McGlone, Research Centre in Brain & Behaviour, Liverpool John Moores University

As a neuroscientist, who for the past 20 years has focussed his research on the skin senses of touch, temperature, pain and itch, the pandemic has had one unwitting beneficial side-effect in that it has alerted us to just how important one particular skin sense is to our social lives and therefore our wellbeing – touch. Only in its absence did people become aware of its subtle presence in their pre-pandemic lives. What recent research has discovered is that we now know we have two touch systems in our skin – a fast one that we have known about for some time that relies on sensory nerves that send signals to the brain in tens of milliseconds, and a recently discovered slow touch system of nerves that send signals to the brain over seconds. The fast one 'senses', the slow one 'feels' and it is this 'feeling' one that is responsible for this more 'subtle' property of touch. The slow touch nerves respond optimally to a gentle caress or hug and when stimulated, release oxytocin and endorphins in the brain and lower heart rate and stress levels. These nerves, called c-tactile afferents *(CTs)*, have been found in the skin of all social mammals and have led to the "skin-as-a-social-organ" hypothesis, which builds on evidence from their role in processing gentle touch, typical of the kind which is common in social interactions.

Although I doubt the writers of **Skin Hunger** knew anything about slow-touch nerves, nonetheless what they have created, with both the context and content of three vignettes played out in the chapel, are intense 'confessions' of how touch has impacted on people's lives. As each actor was ensheathed in a clear plastic cocoon, hanging from the vaulted ceiling of the chapel, a touch barrier separated the actor from the 'audience' as an observer, but this physical separation was punctured as hands 'magically' appeared to penetrate the barrier and offer the experience of sharing physical touch with the actor.

Skin Hunger is a wake-up call to all of us. It is just a shame that it has taken the devastation of a pandemic where for the very first time in 300,000 years of human evolution the 'tactile glue' that holds us together as a social species has been all but dissolved. Touch is the first sense to 'wake up' when we are a mere 10 week old foetus and may well be the last sense to 'go to sleep' when we die, but the role of affective touch – the CT system – in maintaining our physical and mental health across our lives is finally being recognised, as we see and hear from around the planet the anguished calls for "I want a hug".

About Dante or Die

Dante or Die is an award-winning, independent theatre company, led by Daphna Attias and Terry O'Donovan, and produced by Sophie Ignatieff. The company has been creating new performances in unexpected places since 2006. You could experience one of our shows in your local leisure centre or café, the self-storage unit down the road, or on your mobile phone. Creating performances for everyday spaces means that we have the chance to meet new people all the time, to be inspired by stories we wouldn't otherwise hear, and invite people who might not otherwise, to go on a theatrical journey with us.

As Co-Artistic Directors, Daphna and Terry conceive the productions. We put together teams of collaborators and participants specific to each project. They include playwrights and designers as well as leisure centre managers, neuroscientists and people from the communities that we're working in. The creation process is usually a couple of years long, and involves dozens of people, knocking on a lot of doors and many, many surprising conversations. Hundreds of participants have taken part in our productions, and we've run thousands of hours of development workshops and residencies in person, online and as far afield as Hong Kong.

We create partnerships with arts organisations and local businesses and have had the pleasure of collaborating with organisations that we hugely admire such as Almeida Theatre, Traverse Theatre, The Lowry, South Street Reading, BAM New York, Cork Midsummer Festival, Lighthouse Poole, Stone Nest, Ideas Test… This list goes on.

DANTE OR DIE

Original Production Credits

The original production of **Skin Hunger** premiered on 15 June 2021 at Stone Nest in Central London and was performed 72 times over two weeks.

Created by Daphna Attias & Terry O'Donovan

Written by
Ann Akinjirin *(Our Hands)*
Tim Crouch *(The Sessions)*
Sonia Hughes *(Touch The Flesh)*

Directed by Daphna Attias
Performed by
Rachel-Leah Hosker *(Our Hands)*
Terry O'Donovan *(The Sessions)*
Oseloka Obi *(Touch the Flesh)*
Deshaye Gayle *(Understudy)*

Design by Khadija Raza
Additional Design by Jemima Robinson
Music & Sound Design by Yaniv Fridel & Ofer OJ Shabi
Lighting Design by Zia Bergin-Holly
Movement Direction by Ayse Tashkiran
BSL Interpretation by Becky Barry

Produced by Sophie Ignatieff
Production Management by Keegan Curran
Acting Production Management by Danny Cunningham
Stage Management by Jenefer Tait
Assistant Stage Management by Stefy Barton
Front of House Management by Jasmin Hay
Student Placements: Anna T. Stenberg & Sophia Enderby

For Stone Nest: Inna Schorr, Richard Williamson & Hannah Myers

Stone Nest is an arts organisation and performance venue in the heart of London's West End, bringing experimental art to a wide audience. A hidden gem nestled amidst the bright lights of theatreland, offering a platform for bold, visionary artists and a space where audiences can encounter an eclectic programme of contemporary performance. Whilst the 'work in progress' of building restoration continues, we are delighted to collaborate with a range of artists to bring life to this iconic former Welsh chapel, which has its own vibrant social history.

A spiritual home for almost a century, the building played out the hedonistic 80s and 90s as the infamous Limelight nightclub, before its most recent reimagining as Stone Nest. At a time when our need for art, culture and shared experience is greater than ever, we were delighted to collaborate with Dante or Die on **Skin Hunger**, and to open our doors to the public for this timely new work.

www.stonenest.org

Twitter: @StoneNest_LDN

Introduction by Daphna Attias – Co-Artistic Director & Director

A few months into the Covid-19 pandemic, I came across a picture of a hug tunnel in a Brazilian care home. Hug tunnels are plastic curtains with attached plastic arms that allow two people to hug one another safely. They enabled elderly people to hug their loved ones during the pandemic. I immediately sent the picture to my Co-Artistic Director Terry and we agreed that there was a show there. I could instantly picture the chapel in Stone Nest wrapped in plastic. Plastic – a material that had quietly become such an integral part of our lives by covering our faces and hands, creating a barrier between us and the world, becoming a protective layer for so many tactile parts of our everyday. We invited designer Khadija Raza to dream this with us and she created a beautiful installation for audiences to move in, and to touch.

We wanted to invite different voices to contribute. We wondered how this lack of touch, this phenomenon of skin hunger affected different people so we welcomed Ann, Tim & Sonia as writers and gave them a simple task: to write a 10-minute monologue which would in reality be a dialogue between a performer and one audience member and to make the touch an integral part of the narrative. We asked them to explore how touch could be part of the story unfolding. I hadn't met any of them in real life until they came to see the show. We never had a chance to shake hands or hug until after the piece opened and yet we were able to remotely dive into what touch means to all of us. We shared our experiences of caring for aging parents, missing a lost love or fighting for a new start.

I asked composer Yaniv Fridel to compose a piece of music which could be broken into three pieces playing side by side. He focused on each piece using a different instrument – cello, trombone and synthesizer – which came together and apart throughout the show. Three stories, three performers, three audience members, three instruments all playing side by side, all creating a shared composition of intimacy.

I was confronted with new questions: how to direct communication through touch, when to let go of hands and when to squeeze palms, how to touch fingers tip to tip, how to invite someone for a hug and how to constantly allow the audience to have choice and agency and be aware of what they feel comfortable with. Each audience member's limits are different. How can we rehearse a piece that fundamentally changes each time it's performed? We focused on what ifs and studied strategies. In such close proximity to the audience, every breath matters, even the temperature of your hands could change the story.

We were amazed by how vastly different people's reactions were. We constantly adapted the way in which we gave gentle instructions to the audience. Terry whispered into their ear 'is this ok?', Rachel whispered that they could let go at any point and Oseloka reminded them that they could choose either to repeat parts of the text or just listen silently. We learned from audiences what might feel too intimate; like moving hands slowly from one point to another and that a small change like lifting your fingers could make the whole difference. It was a constant process of discovery.

I mostly watched the show from the balcony of Stone Nest. Observed from afar as people accepted or rejected the offers of contact, walked away or didn't want to leave, looked directly into the performer's eyes or found the eye contact too intrusive. Each audience member brought their own story into the show, their own history, limits and fears.

Directing **Skin Hunger** was mostly a process of remembering how we make contact with each other.

A hug tunnel in a Brazilian care home. Photo by Lucas Uebel via Getty Images

The Production

In June 2021 **Skin Hunger** was first performed at Stone Nest, an empty chapel in Central London. Three audience members entered the space every hour, six times a day.

Each audience member followed a route through the space marked out by blue, green and yellow tape. Each route experienced the same three pieces but in a different order.

All three pieces were performed at the same time and repeated three times.

Each one-on-one encounter offered an audience member, who was wearing plastic gloves and a mask, moments of touch through the plastic, which they could accept or not. It was up to them.

The journey to performances was a challenging one. Conceived in the summer of 2020, the original plan was to bring the production to audiences in November 2020. The creative collaborations began on Zoom; meeting researchers and sharing images and inspirations online. We auditioned performers in person, which was a joy following the months of isolation. The UK was split into a tiered system that dictated different levels of social interaction. **Skin Hunger** was legally allowed to be performed within Tier 3. Stage Manager Jen Tait worked tirelessly with the production team to ensure that our plans worked in accordance with the rules, as well as helping audiences to feel safe. It felt exhilarating, daunting and daring.

On Saturday, 31st October the Prime Minister announced a new nationwide lockdown.

All live performances were shut down. We were due to start building the installation on Monday, 2nd November. The production was postponed indefinitely. When it became clearer that we would more than likely be able to perform the piece after the rules relaxed on 17 May 2021, we started putting it all back together. It was a new jigsaw puzzle. The original cast were no longer available. Designer Khadija Raza and Production Manager and Lighting Designer Richard Williamson had clashing commitments and so Jemima Roberts joined as Associate Designer and Zia Bergin-Holly joined as Lighting Designer…..
We began to rebuild, to rehearse with brilliant new actors, to re-prepare for meeting audiences.

This book is a record of this period, with reflections from team members alongside the writing for performance. Each trio of audience members experienced Ann, Tim and Sonia's pieces in a different order. For the purposes of the book we had to put them in an order, so they appear alphabetically. Feel free to read them in any order.

The creative team on a remote development session: Jenefer Tait, Daphna Attias, Ayse Tashkiran, Sonia Hughes, Richard Williamson, Terry O'Donovan, Yaniv Fridel, Khadija Raza, Tim Crouch, Ann Akinjirin

Production Image. Oseloka Obi, Rachel-Leah Hosker & Terry O'Donovan with audience members walking through the space. Image by Justin Jones

The empty chapel at Stone Nest. Image by Valentina Korabelnikova

Khadija Raza's sketch for the Stone Nest installation design.
Image by Khadija Raza

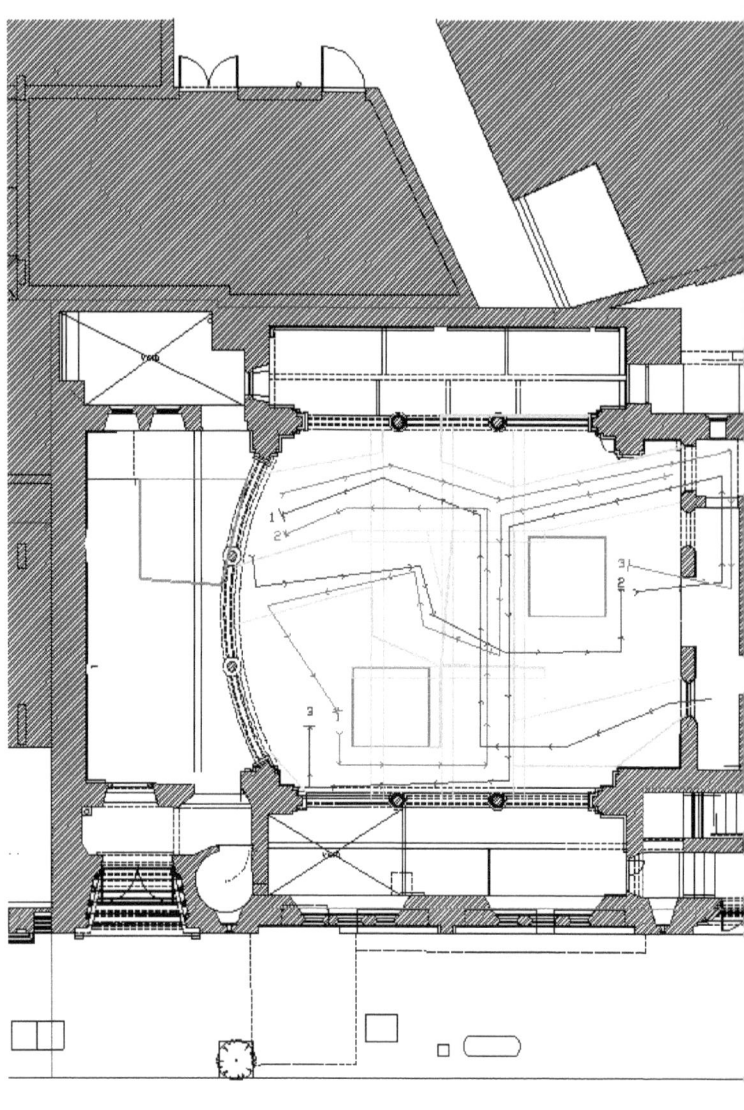

Technical drawing of the installation and audience routes.
Image by Khadija Raza

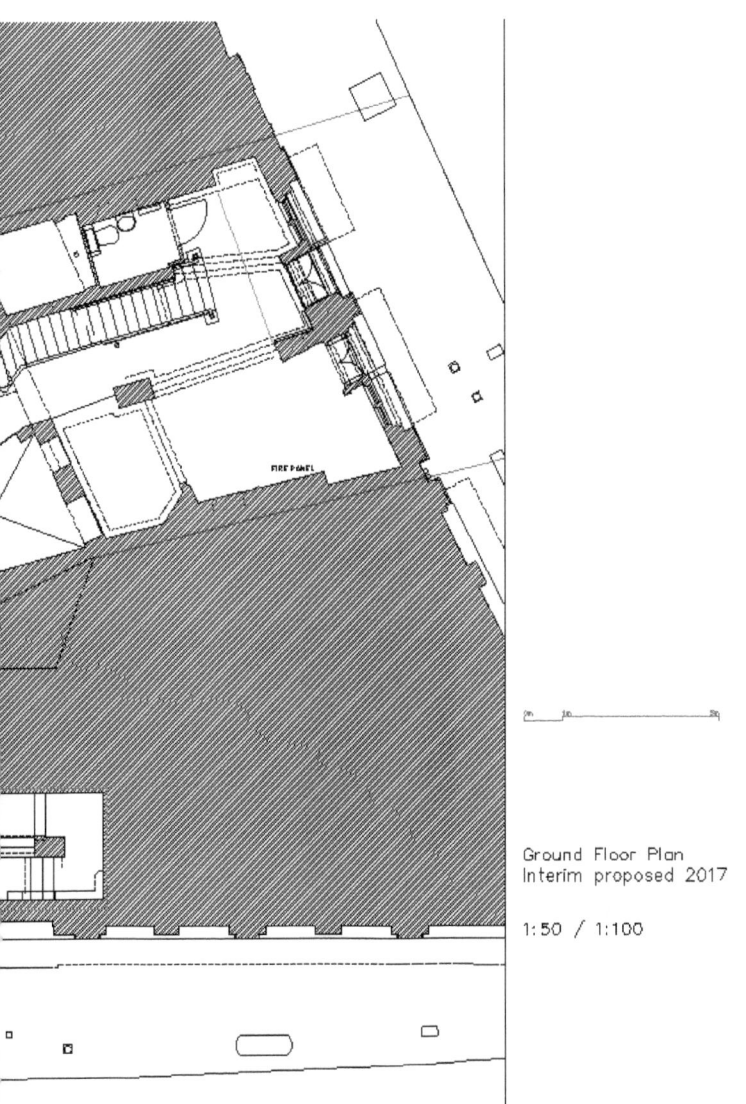

Ground Floor Plan
Interim proposed 2017

1:50 / 1:100

Production image taken from above. Audience members didn't see the installation from above – they walked a blue, green or yellow route as marked on the floor. Oseloka Obi, Rachel-Leah Hosker. Image by Justin Jones

Reflection by Ann Akinjirin – Writer

I was asked to write my piece for **Skin Hunger** just as we were easing out of the first lockdown in the summer of 2020. The first lockdown had a profound effect on me, both positive and negative, for a number of reasons. But, being a Londoner who lives alone, it was at times terribly lonely. I was single during the first lockdown and it was unavoidable to ponder what that means when forced into a national pandemic.

There are so many ways in which we can miss touch and I was very interested in writing about this within the context of love and lost love. It made me think about what I love and missed the most about touch within a relationship and I learned, more specifically, that I missed how your hands interact when you are in love.

As a person who doesn't like being touched unless I'm comfortable, regardless of who the person is, I did struggle slightly with the idea of making an audience member touch the performer. I wondered how I would feel being 'forced' to touch a stranger. I needed to find a way to write the piece where the audience member felt like they had agency to touch when invited.

Watching the piece took me by surprise, it was so brilliantly performed and I wasn't expecting to be so touched by the journey of vulnerability when both falling in and out of love.

Rachel-Leah Hosker holding hands with an audience member whilst performing *Our Hands* by Ann Akinjirin. Image by Justin Jones

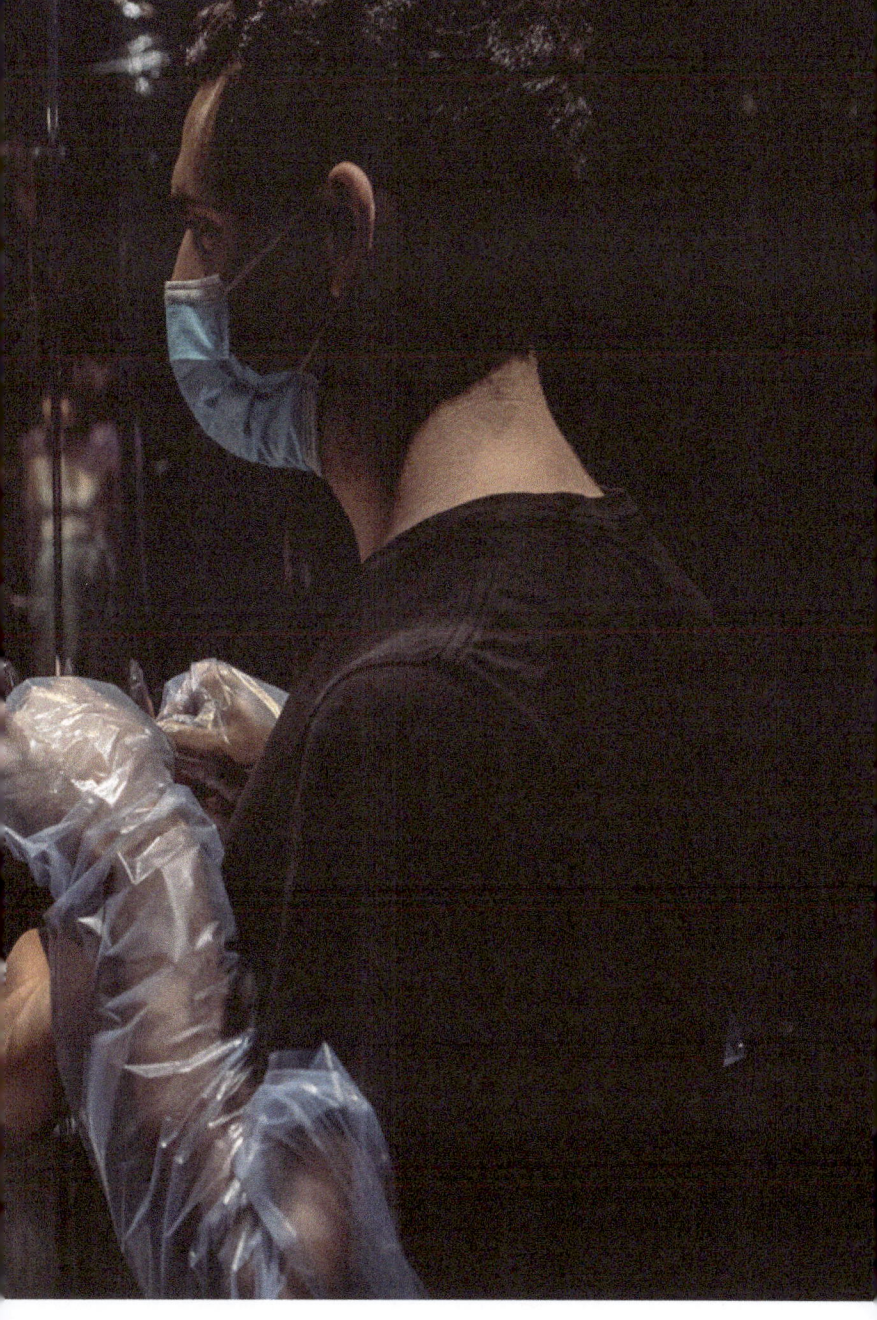

Our Hands by Ann Akinjirin

Do you want to know the body part that I'm most insecure about?
Ummm

I'm actually embarrassed to say, it's silly

But…

It's my hands! I don't have soft hands.

When I was 14, at that age when the shift is happening. That shift, that seemingly overnight shift, where I went from not noticing or frankly giving a fuck what people thought about me to hanging on to every word.

I went to shake someone's hand. In a large group, innocently and politely, I gave them my hand and they flinched. They pulled away so quickly and in front of everyone, at the top of their lungs, they said

"You don't have soft hands!" They asked

"Why are your hands so rough?" And…

I didn't have an answer, because not only did I not know… but I didn't know! I didn't know that my palms weren't soft. It was the first moment I realised that other people must have palms that felt different to mine. That moment the seed was planted that if I offered someone my palm, they may flinch

I was 14 and I've never forgotten

And so the body part that I'm most insecure about isn't my bum or my height or my stomach or whatever the fuck! But it's my hands…

From that moment onwards, every time I fell in lust or love I never wanted people to touch my hands… until I met

You

When we were moving from strangers to lovers, I started my usual dance of avoiding hands. The subtle sway and redirection of my palms when I noticed that your hands were journeying towards mine. But one day, just before I had the chance to move, our palms connected and I froze. I'd perfected these moves over the years and the excuses but you could see through me. You saw into me. You saw me.

"Don't you want to hold my hand?" You asked

My inner 14 year old self looked to the floor. I just couldn't meet your eyes, as I had to admit…

"I don't have soft hands"

You put your hand to my chin. You touched my skin to lift my gaze to yours and you said "You're perfect"

Offers hands

(To audience) You said…

(You're Perfect)

Oh mayn! I was done in from that moment! Finished!

My hands fit yours; I don't want to say like a glove, it's not like that. They fit like… I dunno, snug?

And I was smug about it! So smuggy smug!!

Like my hands were formed to fit perfectly into the gaps between yours and the texture of my palms were made to compliment yours and only yours. They were made for you!

They were just waiting for you Perfect!

I love the journey our hands go on.

The way that, my hands especially, get to love you And how I get to be loved by you through yours.

I love the way you hold my hand

On Sunday mornings we do my favourite thing. We sit on the sofa, silently together, and we read. Seemingly separate but always connected through our hands. I'm touching the nape of your neck and your hand on my knee.

Silent Separate Together

And then we find palms. Your thumb always softly strokes my hand when our fingers are combined

You are so funny. I'm going to be bold and say you're the funniest person I know. We laugh until our stomachs hurt and I curl over, hand to your chest and giggle

Hard

I curl into you and we are enveloped in laughter. Your hand on the back of my head

Laughing Touching Together

And then we hold hands. Our fingers intertwined… I love the way you hold my hand Your face

There's a special way that your face feels on my fingertips

Whenever you're confused your nose wrinkles. I giggle just seeing it in my mind's eye Your nose wrinkles and it gives you away.

My index finger smoothes out your nose with a stroke and you catch yourself

I love the way my fingers can comfort you

Uncomfortable Comfortable Together

I hate being close to people in bed. I don't get how people do it? How do they do it?

I'm so hot and sweaty and I just feel trapped. So I always start in an embrace but then it's like a race for me to see how quickly I can unwind from you as soon as you nod off. But I always awake, always! And find that no matter how far away I am from you in bed your hand would be touching me. Whether it was my back, my legs sometimes even just the tip of my fingers

Tip to tip! Just perfect

Your hand always finds me in bed

Apart Connected Forever

Even when we argue we are touching My impulse is to walk/

To run away

Immediately

Far away

But you grab my hands and you say

"We may be fighting but we have to stay connected I don't want you to let me go!"

You say, "I don't want you to let me go" *(I don't want you to let me go)*

My heart!

I first notice we are drifting apart because our hands aren't meeting

Even when they do, there is something about the way that your hands twist that makes mine feel like they don't fit

They don't fit?

They don't fit yours!

There's something about your energy shift that's making me feel my palm against yours. They don't feel soft anymore

I can feel them

I'd never felt them, with you

But your palms are rejecting mine

Together Touching Resisting

What's happening?

Your hands don't want me like they used to. Are we falling apart?

Our hands aren't touching like they once did My heart?

I miss your hands My hands

Our hands Together

Our hand relationship is changing and it's becoming louder and louder We're falling apart?

My

… heart

I'll never forget that night in bed when I woke; you're on the other side
Back to back

Hands under pillow and nowhere near mine

Your body is stiff, as is mine.

Sleeping

But both awake

Silent

But awake…

And so I whisper "K… are you awake?

Silence "… K…"

"Do you still love me?"

Silence

"… You don't love me anymore"

Silence

Silence…

… Silence

S I L E N C E

"K…"

I whimper

"No…" You reply

You say *(No)*

You say "I don't love you anymore…" *(I don't love you anymore)*

Silence

"Oh…" I say

"Oh… … ok"

Silence

And so you're leaving and I'm watching your hands pack away the love/
The life/

That we had together

I stare as your hands pick up the books that you read beside me on a Sunday

I observed as your fingers pick up the crockery that your hands once washed after dinner

That we made And ate Together

You don't love me anymore?

I look blankly as you try to hand me back your keys

You go to place your hand on my shoulder one last time but I look to the floor. I don't want those hands to leave me

To touch me

Like that

…Loveless

You don't touch me. Your hands hover over my shoulder for what seems like forever and it's like I can feel your touch. I gaze downwards, my tears tapping the wood floor.

But this time your hand doesn't reach my chin to touch me To love me

Love lost

Your Love Has Left Me

Your Hand Won't Touch Me

We can feel the space between your hand and my shoulder We can feel the absence of your touch

And it breaks me

We stay there for a while and then you whisper "Goodbye…"

You say *(Goodbye)*

And your hand shut our/

My door!

No more your door but mine

And I run to it

The door

I touch it

Face to the floor

Hand touching the door I stay there

Forever

Seems like forever

Grieving what we once had

What we once were

What my hand won't feel anymore Knowing that you aren't coming back

Broken Apart Distant

Silence

Silence

Silence…

I run my fingers along cold walls and touch the doorframes of rooms we use to laugh in together

Have you ever noticed the feeling of paper from old books?

I hadn't before now but there's nothing else for me to touch To feel

To notice

On a Sunday

Cold fingers on my face as I look away from the dinner I've made by myself For myself

I don't want to pick up the fork anymore

Don't want to eat alone anymore

I lie in bed now

Palm down in the space that you used to occupy and I'm thinking...

I just...

... I

I just want... I want you

Or someone

I just want someone to hold/ I want my hand to hold/

You/

Someone/

But you! But...

Who's going to hold my hand now?

Will anyone ever hold my hand again?

Reflection by Ayse Tashkiran – Movement Director

Ayse worked across the production from the initial development period through to full production

Our bodies are miraculous. Our capacity to be touched and touch simultaneously gives us a tangled, reciprocal experience of both. It's a truth that you cannot touch without being touched.

Our skin is miraculous: so multifaceted and so big.

Our skin is a map of our experience – constantly renewing and indelibly marked by our lives. Moving with the sensations of our skin and the intelligence of our palms on our own bodies creates haptic circuits that can generate movement. Touch can be laden with memory or catapult us into the here and now of our existence or throw us forward into imagined future possibilities. Who hasn't played out – in their mind's eye – what an embrace will feel like after a long separation? I have….

The space between two strangers in London in June 2021, in the 16th month of a global pandemic is charged and complex. Our pre-pandemic mingling seems like a lifetime ago. As do all those inconsequential, forgettable moments of touch. Acts of hand holding (like the handshake of a stranger) or a finger brush (like a secret message of newly found love) or a stroke (take one hand, trace a line down your arm from the nameless crook of your inner elbow slowly softly gently down to your inner wrist); a road map of soft sensation on a highway of veins to your pulse point.

Moving our intelligent bodies with full expressive capacity suddenly feels like an extraordinary risk and joy. Movement directors dream about all this all the time and then sometimes you are lucky enough to play a part in work that lets you release your wonder of skin, and the subtlety of touch…and create with actors movement material, that then moves and encounters audiences body to body…..

Slip / Brush / Tingle / Wash / Press / Scratch / Glide / Snag / Pat / Stretch / Reach / Rebound / Retreat / Flinch / Hold / Hold Hold…Release

Rehearsals in Stone Nest. The cast and creative team during a notes session

Reflection by Tim Crouch – Writer

There's a thing on social media called #LoveTheatreDay. It's a day when people post uplifting photos of shows, themselves in shows, shows, more shows. I can't subscribe to the sentiment of that hashtag as I have a lot of problems with theatre. It's those problems that keep me in it. They're really good problems. They're human problems. #LoveTheatreProblemsDay

Those problems are central to my **Skin Hunger** piece. The pandemic gave theatre a chance to reset; to gain a new perspective from a period of suspension and reflection. **Skin Hunger** marked the return to live performance after 15 months – an actor meeting their audience again after a long separation. It was the nature of this reunion that prompted the text I wrote – the wider significance of that encounter also becoming the story told in the exchange. I wrote an actor apologising for theatre's past behaviour and I enjoyed the implied overlap with a couple (whose relationship has taken a break) reuniting.

'I will be different next time… ask permission… seek consent… be less intimidating… be truthful… consider you… share the space… look you in the eyes… I won't keep you in the dark next time… I won't shout all the time – next time.'

These are some of the problems I perceive in the human relationship of theatre. The first words the audience member speaks to the actor are *'Shut up'*. And yet the actor keeps obsessing. Promising change, but they keep on talking. Later, the audience gives further advice – *'stop trying so hard'* – but still the actor persists. The act of touch, of holding, is offered as a calming device to settle the actor's needy, nervous energy. But any self-awareness is lost in a return to bad habits.

'The simplicity of waking up in the morning and not having to remember the lies I told the night before. This period of honesty without – with no echo – has been – has been a complete revelation to me. I have changed. Thank you.'

In the writing, it felt like I was exploring a personal manifesto towards a theatre that is honest, balanced and nurturing – a good human relationship. But there's a difference between what the writer sees in their head and how it's received in the world. Watching the work in performance, my neat metaphorical conceit was quickly outstripped by the literal, word-for-word immediacy of human contact. Terry, the performer, looks at me and I see a person, not an idea. All my figures-of-speech disappear into a man who wants me back, who wants me to hold him, to help him, to absolve him. A man whose touch becomes clingy, whose neediness demands reassurance which I'm not entirely sure I want to give. There's no allegory here. My subtle critique is lost in a snarl of human entanglement. Flesh and blood overtaking my concept. I know the idea is still in there somewhere but I'm delighted that it has been overwhelmed by what's in front of my face.

Terry O'Donovan hugging an audience member whilst performing *The Sessions* by Tim Crouch. Image by Justin Jones

The Sessions by Tim Crouch

As they (the audience member) enter this part.

The performer. Restless. Agitated.

The words do the thinking.

(Play with this:) Hi, hi, hi, hi, hi, hi, hi, tell-me-to-shut-up, hi, hi, hi, hi, hi, tell-me-to-shut-up, hi, hi, hi, hi, tell-me-to-shut-up, hi, hi, *etc.*

They, the audience (sooner or later): Shut up.

That's harsh, hard, harsh – hard to hear, to – but fair, I'd say, yes, fair, yes, tonally, totally, I mean, totally *(and tonally)* understandable. Every way yes and. Yes, and I know, I know, I get it, I'm sorry, I'm sorry – own worst – new footing, new – I'll shut up, I'll – shut up.

A moment.

Off again. Fast.

Only, it's just, I was just – you know, and – you know – just was, well I was, was – I am overwhelmed to – I didn't think I – you would – didn't think I'd. See. You. Like this, I mean, in the – Thought you'd never want to – Ever – Again, even, ever, given all we – not we – I – I – After all this – this separation. And you just carrying on, just, just getting on with your life and being brilliant and adapting and working it out and staying in and quietly fixing things, and me obsessing, obsessed, banging on – with the plugged pulled, with some existential fucking world class navel-gazing – me, me, me – this time, this distance. Me. And here you are in real life and I thought that was it – gone for ever – that you would understand that you can manage – without me – *can* manage without me, Jesus, of course – but that the muscle had wasted through lack of use – and then I see you coming in here like nothing's changed and maybe it's not – here you are! – looking like that – and then, like that, the possibility opens like that –

A moment.

You look fucking amazing.

Through all this.

Off again. Fast.

So, this is – for me, for me, you know, it's brilliant. And I'm – sorry, as I said in the sessions. I'm sorry. I'm sorry. And I will be different next time, I promise. And I will listen next time. And I will ask permission next time. And I will seek consent next time. And I will be gentle next time. And I will be less intimidating next time. And I will be truthful to you next time. And I will consider you next time. And I will look you in the eyes next time. And I will share the space next time. And I will make a real connection next time. And I won't keep you in the dark next time. And I won't shout all the time – next time. And I would like to start again with you if that's – if that's – but different – I will be different – and no amount of me smiling and or, or, or posturing or play-acting or turning on the charm or trying to pretend, to pretend it didn't – didn't happen. It *did* happen and it was probably as bad as you remember it and the distance was real but it's in the past and I'm sorry.

Slowly. Would you? Start slowly. Different. Again.

One hand up to the plastic.

Begin again – would you? Can you bear, even? – a hand, even, maybe, just a hand maybe, one touch. I would understand if – With your permission. We restart, maybe? Would you? Say: maybe. Maybe? Say? Maybe?

They, the audience (sooner or later): Maybe.

A hand from them on the other side of the plastic. Hands connected. A moment of calm and breath.

They stay connected through the plastic.

(Play with this:) Thank you thank you thank you thank you.

Space.

Breathe.

I'm sorry.

Space. Hands still connected. Intimate.

In the sessions, remember, they said no expectations, no – tenderly. To create a – tenderness. To reconnect. To open up. As though we didn't – like we never – like some childish role play, remember, would you? like strangers. Like new to each other, like 'hello, what's *your* name' I thought I'd blown it completely, tonally, totally but here you are and there is such hope here.

A beat.

Hello. I'm Terry *(actor should use their own name here)*. What's *your* name?

They (sooner or later) give their name.

Yes.

Hands disconnect.

A moment.

Off again, still fast but a little less agitated.

Fuck, and I know I can be such a fucking black hole sometimes, such an attention seeker sometimes, such a fucking clown – but you here today means everything and I know – I know it's not possible to put it all behind us, to clean the slate completely, to remove all trace of what happened – before – of the – my ingrained – my ingrained behaviours and my – past form – and I said when we were – in the sessions, I said, remember, that I would learn, had learnt, to, to, to recognise the patterns, the abusive – no, not abuse, I challenge that word because it implies a conscious – but the – the unthinking, *my* unthinking – habits – my instincts – that you once found so endearing, that you so delighted in, endorsed, applauded even – once – and you said, in the sessions, you said that you would be prepared to – to consider to – to contemplate even – if I was better – became better – if I – to start again. And then all communication – from you – all sessions – stopped.

The performer's two hands up to the plastic.

And I know that I can be unbearable sometimes – overbearing – and too loud sometimes, too fake sometimes and – and that that knowledge is never enough in itself, in my head – that comprehension that I can be – that I am and was – but I am trying. I am trying – I have a lot of distance to make up – years of blocked – of blocking – and I will try. I will try. Just something to calm me down. Would you, yes? You would, yes? Say, yes? 'Yes', yes?

They, the audience (sooner or later): Yes.

Two hands from the other side of the plastic. Hands touching. A moment of calm and breath. The moment explored.

Thank you.

How do you do that?

Hands still together:

You don't know what this means – it means so – to have this, this, this, this, this – like a ground – for my air, my restless air – for that part of my brain that won't – and I should be able to do this on my own, to find this on my – but I can't, I can't – and I don't need to put on a show for you, do I? That's the point, isn't it? I mean, that's been the whole point. Why haven't I trusted? Just an inveterate – No one ever told me. No. Didn't listen. If someone – you – had said at the start, just said, stop trying so hard. Just said to me, stop trying so hard. Stop trying so hard, said. Say that.

They, the audience (soon or later): Stop trying so hard.

The simplicity of waking up in the morning and not having to remember the lies I told the night before. This period of honesty without – with no echo – has been – has been a complete revelation to me. I have changed. Thank you.

Breathe.

Hands apart.

A moment.

Calmer. Stiller.

I would like to acknowledge the need that put me here. That brought me here. And you here, too, I imagine, although I wouldn't – That we are closer than we are not close. And that the distance has been of my making but you had a hand – And it is not something for either of us to be ashamed of – you, my twin, my better half.

And I can't hope to recreate – because of what has gone before – recreate what we had because it wasn't –could never be – is just the beginning.

If you wanted to hold me. If you wanted to hold me. Hold me and tell me it's okay, to hold me and say it's okay, then I promise– I promise.

They, the audience (sooner or later) hold the performer and say: It's okay.

(Held. Intimate. Settled.)

How do you do that? How does that work? I don't deserve you. I love you. I'm so fucking needy. God, I'm so – but that's not, that's not – it's a force of habit, a tick, an emotional – but this, this is real, isn't it – real?

And I am better, I think, yes, thank you, I'm better. I mean – is it possible to go through what we have been through and not, in some small way, some small, small – be stronger at least? adaptable? – adapt to it – gain some perspective on it from where we are now, here, standing here. I'm sorry. You told me to shut up and I haven't stopped running my mouth – I haven't – I'm sorry. You go. If you would – are prepared to – not take me back – not that, but – safely – on your terms, your conditions – with time to think – I would, will promise to just need less. Want less. Need. Less.

They separate.

Reflection by Terry O'Donovan – Co-Artistic Director & Performer

Over two weeks in June 2021 I performed The Sessions to – and with – 216 audience members.

I can tell that you're smiling from above your mask – the lines around your eyes lifting.

We share a 'hello'.

Your eyes dart around, flick away but jump back to lock into mine. To focus on what I'm trying to say.

You start to get it and get into it.

You lean in.

You move away.

Your eyes become wary.

Your eyes laugh.

Your eyes fill with tears. I want to offer you a tissue but that's not allowed in the current world. When I hug you, you really let me hug you.

When I say the word consent your eyes widen and your body stiffens. You refuse my invitation to touch fingers through the plastic sheet.

You say 'I don't need to listen to this' and you walk away. Two minutes later you return. 'I had a boyfriend who sounded exactly like that and I just couldn't stand to listen to you.'

You explore my hand. My fingers are thinner than yours.

My hand is colder than yours. Your hands warm up my cold hands.

Your nails have different colours. I wonder why you chose those colours.

Your body starts to brim with anger. You shake your head no when I ask you to hold my hands. I feel like I have been monstrous and that you have a deep hatred for me. 'In my experience people like you don't change.'

Your baby bump massively ups the stakes. My fight for forgiveness takes on a whole new meaning.

You hold my hands tightly.

You barely touch my hands at all.

You stroke my palms – nobody does that except my husband. You're trying to calm me down. I'm not sure if you know you're doing it.

You hover your fingers above mine – dangling touch near me but not ready to connect.

You look down at my hands, shake your head slightly, take a deep breath and take the plunge. I wonder if this is the first time you've held hands with another man.

You weep as I hold you tightly. I don't say the lines. It doesn't feel right. I just hold you for a short while. Then we go back to the script.

You rub my back and tell me it's ok. I believe you.

You hold me very tightly. Like I might disappear if you don't hold me that tight. It's a little claustrophobic.

You tell me 'This is goodbye.'

Each of you approached our exchange with your own stories, your own experiences. I was blown away by how present you were and how alive our twelve minutes together were. I hadn't expected you to become so invested in our story. Despite me saying the same words to all 216 of you, our story was different every time.

Reflection by Sonia Hughes – Writer

Last Sunday was Father's Day. My cousin and my sister rang me a couple of days before to ask, would I be alright on Father's Day, would it be tough? No, I said.

Last Sunday was sunny and I'd been rehearsing for my new project the week before so I was kind of tired. I spent most of the day in the garden. I bought myself a new stool, just for gardening, I can't kneel for long, so I have a stool to squat on to mooch about the raised beds. I didn't actually do much gardening, I just sat on the stool or the bench looking. At the plants, the leaves, the stalks, the flowers, the greens, the bees, the sky, the garden. For quite long time. My eyes gently alighting on single things and then the whole then back to mini vistas.

I now understand why my Dad used to do this. How much calm joy can be solicited from sitting in the garden you make. I can see him on the little wooden bench next to his hibiscus shrub opposite his plum tree. Sitting. Looking. Drawing on his treasure.

This is a piece of writing about writing. My dad was living with me. He had Alzheimer's. I experienced it. I wrote about it. I wonder if I should feel guilty. I've put him in public in his most dilapidated state. I've put him in public before with *My Dad Made Cars*. Not so much, he wasn't standing there with his arse out.

Oseloka Obi holding the hand of an audience member whilst performing *Touch the Flesh* by Sonia Hughes. Image by Justin Jones

Touch the Flesh by Sonia Hughes

One slipper on. Side together side, step. Side together side, step, as if coming down the stairs.

Sung: I'm coming down… I'm coming down, I want the world to know, I'm coming down. [*Diana Ross – I'm coming out*]

Oh. You remember me?

Puts his bare hand out of a hole.

Touch the flesh.

Touch the flesh nah?

Withdraws his hand. Sniffs. Pats his pockets, searches his pockets. Sniffs. Squeezes his nose. Pats his pockets, searches his pocket.

Have you got… have you got something *squeezes his nose .. . he pulls out the lining of his pocket, it is not a handkerchief,* something for my nose, *he points at an object,* is that any good for my nose, *he makes contact with the plastic sheet, uses the plastic sheet to blow his nose.* Not that. *He searches his pocket. He notices you again, as if for the first time.*

How was, how was the, the … pageant? You enjoy it?

There was a lot of people there?

He sees a shitty piece of tissue on the floor. He goes to pick it up. | Not that! Not that Dad, it's dirty.

| *He is still bending to reach it.*

| Don't pick it up. I'll do it. You're meant to put it in the toilet, why don't you put in the toilet when you're done. *She gets a tissue out of her pocket and picks the dirty tissue up, disposes of it.*

| Sorry, sorry.

| *She takes another tissue out of her pocket.*

| *He blows his nose and puts the tissue in his pocket.* Sorry *(as in excuse me)*

Well, well, well. So long since I see you. How are the children? Good to see you, good to see you. *He thrusts his bare hand out of the hole.* Touch the flesh nah man.

| Yeah, sorry he doesn't get the whole… Sorry I'm Oseloka*, I'm from Hackney but I'm down here for a few weeks doing this. What's your name?

You answer.

Repeats the name. You're meant to repeat the name as soon as possible that way it sticks. Doesn't work, I mean I won't remember but just as a friendly gesture, actually I can remember the person before you was x, and the one before them was y. it says x and y in the script but I think the intention was for me to say the last couple of audience member's names, but honestly – gone. But I'm okay with faces. Like I could see you in the street later and I'd think yeah, she was in the show this afternoon, but name, no gone, nothing.

| You see the pack of cards?

Some men came and they say, they want me to bring me the, the *rubs his fingers with his thumb, then looks down and clicks his fingers, and clicks his fingers again.*

| A pack of cards? What cards?

| Yes. The men came and they want, *he points repeatedly at something, tugs his jumper, clicks his finger, looks down. Looks up expectantly at you.*

| Which men dad?

Don't worry about it. No one's coming at this time of night. If they come back, I'll find out what they want.

| Never mind. If they come –

| Just go back to bed.

| *He laughs.* I'm not going to bed. I got to go home now.

| Oh okay. I thought you were staying with me for a while.

| *Laughs.* No I going home, the children will wonder what happened to me. | What children?

| I got two little girls, Sonia-

| I'm Sonia. I'm Sonia and you're my Dad.

| *He looks at her, then looks at you.* You bring you car? You could take me? | This is my home, and you're staying here with me, Dad.

| *Laughs. Looks at you.* Are you the taxi? You could take me home? 36 Buckwood Avenue.

| Actually, she's sold the house. On his 90th birthday she sold the house out from under him, he has no idea. To be fair he no longer realised it was his home, although he'd been in that house 60 years. She didn't take much, a really good baking tray, the bread board, brand new towels. There was a few sentimental things the reel to reel tape recorder, her dead brother's t-shirt, a bundle of birthday cards. They'll go in a box, for what, what's she going to do with them? Make another show? The things she really wanted was the trees he'd planted. The apple tree in the corner especially.

| *Sings loudly* So I'll cherish the old rugged cross, till my trophies at last I lay down, I will cling to the old rugged cross and replace it one day for a crown.

I going home, you hear?

He walks up and down the plastic, looking for a way out. Singing. I will cling to the old rugged cross…

| You can't go out now, you only have one slipper on. | No, look I have my shoes. *He points to his feet.*

| No that's a sock, you need both slippers on. This one is a slipper *she touches his slippered foot,* but this one is just a slipper. *She touches his foot with the sock on.*

| *He looks at his feet.* Yeah. Well, look at that. You could get me the other slipper?

| It's wet, it needs washing, you peed in it.

| *Laughs* what you talking about, how I could do that?

| You do it all the time.

| *Laughs* you think I foolish.

| Yes! Yes, you are foolish, you are dad. you have Alzheimer's and you wee in your slipper!

| Look it there. *He points to his slipper on the audience side of the plastic.* Can you? *He points, he points at his feet, he looks at you.*

| *Oseloka points at the slipper.* Give it to him, it's best if he feels that no-one is stopping him. No really it's fine, it's been sanitised between each round. Honestly, or get a glove,

| *sings,* I will cling to the old rugged cross.

| thanks. Yes, it is wet it's been sprayed with the clean thing, it's not wee I promise you. Smell it. *It smells of urine.*

| *He walks back up the stairs. Side together side, step. Side together side, step. He walks down the stairs.*

Reciting. Oh, who are the weary pilgrims? Tis the women with market burdens and their hampered donkeys… and their hampered donkeys… Can't bring it. *laughs.* Me head no good.

| *She claps,* That's great. *She claps.* That's great Dad.

He laughs You seen my Mom? | No.

| You don't see her?

Look her there.

| *She shakes her head.* | Mom? Mom.

| It's not clear here whether he's talking about his Mum or his wife. Sometimes he conflates the two. There's a picture of them that she/I has/have and it had been on their bedroom wall forever at 36 Buckwood Avenue, their heads are inclined and they are nearly smiling, when he sees it now he says 'look there, me mother and father.' Below it there's a picture of him reciting a poem at my wedding. He doesn't remember that he came to the wedding. It's nearly all gone now. There used to be little glimpses of him.

| *She looks into your eyes/ He holds your gaze.* Where is he? Hefting full sacks of potatoes, double digging the vegetable patch in your 80s. 'Come on

nah man, you mus' have a drink.' Picking blackberries to make jam with Mum, barefoot on wet morning grass. Chat up the ladies. Tailor me a pair of trousers. Wield a hammer to defend our home. You hung out with the young men and cared for old ladies… | *Oseloka holds your gaze.* He's nowhere on this earth. He's dead. Between the last draft of this scene and this one, he died. He's a jar of ashes in the undertaker's cupboard.

Oseloka looks at you and smiles. We'll do the death scene. *Oseloka readies himself.*

| *His breathing is laboured, his eyes closed, he is still apart from his chest rising and falling, his mouth is open. This is more than a demonstration. Oseloka stops and starts till he does it as well as he can.*

| She is holding his hand. *Puts his hand through the plastic sleeve, encourages you to hold his hand.* | *The breathing again* | *whilst stroking his/your arm and gauging how it is being received, sings* The Lord's My Shepherd, I'll not want, he makes me down to lie, in pastures green, he leadeth me, the quiet waters by. *Checks.* My soul he doth restore again -

You can go now. There's nothing else for you to do, Dad. I love you. I love you my darling Dad. | *Last breath out.*

| That's not how the previous draft ended, *Oseloka takes back his arm,* she said something about holding her son as a child, then some confusion and he finishes it with | there's a fella want me help go pick mango. | The ending's raggedy now.

Oh, okay. Stage direction. She washes his body then dresses him, but forgets to give him a clean handkerchief. Yeah, that's it.

*actor should use their own name

Terry O'Donovan and an audience member hug during *The Sessions* by Tim Crouch. Image by Justin Jones

Reflection from The Audience

'I felt like I was really in the room and being asked something real about how we interact. You made me laugh and cry and question what touch I give and receive.'

'I wasn't expecting to cry, least not in each performance. Maybe it's because I live on my own and was less used to human contact over the past year? Maybe it's because it was very intimate? Or maybe it was the direct eye contact and very personal individual experience. I felt obliged to touch. I didn't necessarily always want to – but with experience of performing myself I empathised with the position of the actor and felt obliged to play along.'

'It's quite hard on the audience actually. But really interesting as we totally become the person to whom they are talking. We are in the text. It's very moving.'

'In a lifetime of theatre-going, this must be my most intimate experience. After fifteen months of limited contact and little live theatre, the one-on-one experience was initially challenging, but the connection with the characters and their stories proved to be captivating.'

'I felt special. Being able to go on the journey by myself, without having to share the performers attention, was great. I laughed, I cried, I questioned their words and actions and that freedom of knowing no other audience members would see me, or judge me was freeing.'

'It was profoundly and disturbingly, both tactile and insubstantial at the same time. The plastic curtains looked fantastic with the light reflected off them, as if they went into the skies or firmaments; they created a space for another world, similar to ours but separate. This was a world that reflected ours, connected to it, but didn't blend or overlap. The touching was discomforting – I was reluctant to hug – I hadn't hugged a friend for fifteen months and the plastic only emphasised our recent distance to each other. The feeling was very contradictory.'

'This was the first theatre show I'd seen since Corona started. The intimacy and intensity has really stayed in my mind. There were moments where I forgot I was in a show and I was simply witnessing another human's story.'

'Conflicted whether to hug and touch the apologetic partner, I changed position of my hands to feel more in control. At the same time, it felt good just to be so close to another human! Holding hands with the dying father became a profound moment for me to say goodbye to my own father who passed away suddenly recently and this touch felt cathartic and healing in a moment of grief.'

www.salamanderstreet.com

www.ingramcontent.com/pod-product-compliance
Ingram Content Group UK Ltd.
Pitfield, Milton Keynes, MK11 3LW, UK
UKHW060844160426
5217IPUK00042B/2080